DATE DUE			

Of QUARKS, QUASARS, AND OTHER QUIRKS
Quizzical Poems for the Supersonic Age

Of QUARKS, QUASARS, AND OTHER QUIRKS
Quizzical Poems for the Supersonic Age

COLLECTED BY

Sara and John E. Brewton and John Brewton Blackburn

Illustrated by Quentin Blake

THOMAS Y. CROWELL · NEW YORK

Library of Congress Cataloging in Publication Data. Main entry under title: Of quarks, quasars, and other quirks. Includes indexes. SUMMARY: A collection of poems dealing with such aspects of modern life as computers, atomic bombs, space travel, transplants, and pollution. 1. Children's poetry. [1. Civilization, Modern—Poetry] I. Brewton, Sara Westbrook. II. Brewton, John Edmund, 1898-. III. Blackburn, John Brewton. IV. Blake, Quentin. PN6110.C4035   808.81   76-54747   ISBN 0-690-01286-1 ISBN 0-690-04885-8 (lib. bdg.)

10 9 8 7 6 5

ACKNOWLEDGMENTS

Grateful acknowledgment is made to the following publishers, authors, and other copyright holders for permission to reprint copyrighted material:

ABINGDON PRESS for "Unless We Guard Them Well" from Because It's Here by Jane Merchant, copyright © 1970 by Jane Merchant.

RICHARD ARMOUR for "Deus ex Machina" from Light Armour by Richard Armour, copyright © 1954 by Richard Armour, published by McGraw-Hill Book Company.

ATHENEUM PUBLISHERS for "Teevee" from Catch a Little Rhyme by Eve Merriam, copyright © 1966 by Eve Merriam; "A Charm for Our Time," and "Think Tank" from Out Loud by Eve Merriam, copyright © 1973 by Eve Merriam; and "Only a Little Litter" from The Malibu and Other Poems by Myra Cohn Livingston (a Margaret K. McElderry Book), copyright © 1972 by Myra Cohn Livingston. Used by permission of Atheneum Publishers.

To the memory of Sara Westbrook Brewton

Books Compiled by John E. Brewton

Under the Tent of the Sky
Gaily We Parade
Poetry Time

With Sara Brewton

Christmas Bells Are Ringing
Bridled with Rainbows
Sing a Song of Seasons
Birthday Candles Burning Bright
Laughable Limericks
America Forever New
    A Book of Poems
Shrieks at Midnight
    Macabre Poems, Eerie and Humorous
Index to Children's Poetry
Index to Children's Poetry
    First Supplement
Index to Children's Poetry
    Second Supplement

With Sara Brewton and G. Meredith Blackburn III

Index to Poetry for Children and Young People
My Tang's Tungled
    And Other Ridiculous Situations

Contents

Blast Off!   1

Relax. It's Sonic Boom.   17

Modern Science Makes Its Mark   29

Where the Neuter Computer Goes *Click*   49

Bless Our Modern Castle   63

I'm Lost Among a Maze of Cans   81

Progress Takes Its Toll, I'm Told   89

Index of Titles   107

Index of First Lines   109

Index of Authors   112

PROGRESS

Scientists are now seeking tiny particles even smaller than electrons from which they believe all matter is built. These basic building blocks are called "quarks."—news item

Once we felt at home with Nature if we knew the
    nomenclature
Of a dozen trees and flowers in the park.
She was then our own dear girlie, but she turned arcane and
    surly
From the moment modern science made its mark.

If we try to sing her praises in the old familiar phrases
    She says "Blast off!" in response to "Hark! the lark!"
And requires us to dote on the electron and the proton
    While we're foundering bewildered in the dark.

So we strain to get in orbit with this science and absorb it
    With the glimmer of a comprehending spark,
But we've barely got the laser separated from the maser
    When we're thrown into the hunting of the quark.

Felicia Lamport

BLAST OFF!

from PROGRESS

If we try to sing her praises in the old familiar phrases
  She says "Blast off!" in response to "Hark! the lark!"
And requires us to dote on the electron and the proton
While we're foundering bewildered in the dark.

—Felicia Lamport

TIME OF THE MAD ATOM

This is the age
Of the half-read page.
And the quick hash
And the mad dash.
The bright night
With the nerves tight.
The plane hop
And the brief stop.
The lamp tan
In a short span.
The Big Shot
In a good spot.
And the brain strain
And the heart pain.
And the cat naps
Till the spring snaps—
And the fun's done!

Virginia Brasier

INTERPLANETARY LIMERICKS

A Martian named Harrison Harris
Decided he'd like to see Paris;
    In space (so we learn)
    He forgot where to turn—
And that's why he's now on Polaris.

By rocket, to visit the moon,
Went song writer Hannibal Boone;
    He wasn't there long
    Before writing a song
Called Earth Over Luna Lagoon.

The ladies inhabiting Venus
Have signalled us saying they've seen us;
    They add, "There's a yen here
    For getting some men here—
And nothing but space is between us!"

Al Graham

from THE SPACE CHILD'S MOTHER GOOSE

1

Probable-Possible, my black hen,
She lays eggs in the Relative When.
She doesn't lay eggs in the Positive Now
Because she's unable to Postulate How.

5

Little Bo-Peep
Has lost her sheep,
The radar has failed to find them.
They'll all, face to face,
Meet in parallel space,
Preceding their leaders behind them.

10

This little pig built a spaceship,
This little pig paid the bill;
This little pig made isotopes,
This little pig ate a pill;
And this little pig did nothing at all,
But he's just a little pig still.

22

Solomon Grundy
Walked on Monday
Rode on Tuesday
Motored Wednesday

Planed on Thursday
Rocketed Friday
Spaceship Saturday
Time Machine Sunday
Where is the end for
Solomon Grundy?

Frederick Winsor

FASTER THAN LIGHT

There was a young lady named Bright,
Whose speed was much faster than light.
    She went out one day
    In a relative way
And returned on the previous night.

A. H. Reginald Buller

SAME OLD TRICK

When a missile goes over the moon, I'm a guy
    Who can read the report without arching a brow;
Though a jump such as that is remarkably high,
    It was done long ago by a common old cow.

William W. Pratt

S F

From my city bed in the dawn I
    see a raccoon
On my neighbor's roof.
He walks along in his wisdom in the
    gutter,
And passes from view
On his way to his striped
    spaceship to doff his disguise
And return to Mars
As a Martian
Raccoon.

Ernest Leverett

RELATIVITY

"The world is such a funny place,"
  Remarked a topsy-turvy Ace,
    A-sliding down a curve in space,

"But, from this angle I can see
  No gently sloping theory,
    I am inclined toward Gravity,

"And even Einstein would compute
  That Time and Space are both *Acute*
    When dropping in a parachute!"

                    Kathleen Millay

FAR TREK

Some things will never change although
We tour out to the stars;
Arriving on the moon we'll find
Our luggage sent to Mars!

                    June Brady

CAPSULE PHILOSOPHY

*The psychological effects of space flight cannot be
known, according to Navy psychologists, until a man is
actually in space.*—news item

Can a mere human brain stand the stress and the strain
   That were strictly designed for the birds?
When a man's face to face with remote outer space
   Is he likely to chirp or use words?

Will he hanker and yearn for a rapid return
   To the home of his kith and his kin
Or, when gravity snaps, will this unwonted lapse
   Send him straight to the great lunar bin?

Felicia Lamport

ASTRONAUT'S CHOICE

The scientists sit long of nights
Over their weighty calculations—
How to put a man in space,
Clothe him, warm him, feed him rations,
Bring him safely back to earth
By well-planned decelerations.

How is it that they do not see
There is a graver risk by far?
Perhaps with atom bombs and taxes
And world crises as they are,
Their astronaut may choose to settle
Down upon the farthest star.

                                    M. M. Darcy

ONLY A LITTLE LITTER

Hey moonface,
    man-in-the-moonface,

    do you like the way
    we left your place?

    can you stand the view
    of footprints on you?

    is it fun to stare
    at the flags up there?

    did you notice ours
    with the stripes and stars?

    does it warm you to know
    we love you so?

moonface,
man-in-the-moonface,

thanks a heap for the rocks.

Myra Cohn Livingston

MOON POEM

"Ouu
gee whiz
hey charlie
look
purple rocks
hey alan
over here
looks like glass
got to have
one of these
just like green glass
ouu get one of those. . . ."

You'all better leave God's moon alone,
Else he ain't gonna turn it on, no more!

Saundra Sharp

NOT LOST IN THE STARS

Said the engineer, "Radio waves
Go in all directions, and until stopped,
Continue forever."
So there are billions of them
Reaching trillions of miles into the icy blackness
Among the quasars and the pulsars.
"Keep your breath sweet all day."
"They won't marry you if you perspire."
"Bunions are off, with Bunoff."
The depths of inconceivable space
Are getting the hard sell,
Making dying worlds glad to go,
And saddening those waiting to be born.

Bruce Bliven

VALENTINE FOR EARTH

Oh, it will be fine
To rocket through space
And see the reverse
Of the moon's dark face,

To travel to Saturn
Or Venus or Mars,
Or maybe discover
Some uncharted stars.

But do they have anything
Better than we?
Do you think, for instance,
They have a blue sea
For sailing and swimming?
Do planets have hills
With raspberry thickets
Where a song sparrow fills

The summer with music?
And do they have snow
To silver the roads
Where the school buses go?

Oh, I'm all for rockets
And worlds cold or hot,

But I'm wild in love
With the planet we've got!

Frances Frost

15

RELAX.
IT'S SONIC BOOM.

from SONIC BOOM

I'm sitting in the living room,
When, up above, the Thump of Doom
Resounds. Relax. It's sonic boom.

—John Updike

SONIC BOOM

I'm sitting in the living room,
When, up above, the Thump of Doom
Resounds. Relax. It's sonic boom.

The ceiling shudders at the clap,
The mirrors tilt, the rafters snap,
And Baby wakens from his nap.

"Hush, babe. Some pilot we equip,
Giving the speed of sound the slip,
Has cracked the air like a penny whip."

Our world is far from frightening; I
No longer strain to read the sky
Where moving fingers (jet planes) fly.
Our world seems much too tame to die.

And if it does, with one more pop,
I shan't look up to see it drop.

John Updike

ANY DAY NOW

Johnny reading in his comic
Learned to handle the atomic.
Johnny blew us all to vapors.
What a lad for cutting capers.

David McCord

ATOMIC COURTESY

To smash the simple atom
All mankind was intent.
  Now any day
  The atom may
Return the compliment.

Ethel Jacobson

35

The Hydrogen Dog and the Cobalt Cat
Side by side in the Armory sat.
Nobody thought about fusion or fission
Everyone spoke of their peacetime mission,
  Till somebody came and opened the door.
There they were, in a neutron fog,
The Codrogen Cat and the Hybalt Dog;
  They mushroomed up with a terrible roar—
  And Nobody Never was there—Nomore.

Frederick Winsor

MOTHER GOOSE
(*Circa 2054*)

Humpty Dumpty sat on the wall,
A non-electro-magnet ball.
All the Super's polariscopes
Couldn't revitalize his isotopes.

Irene Sekula

from A LEADEN TREASURY
OF ENGLISH VERSE

1

Ring-a-ring o' neutrons,
A pocket full of positrons.
A fission! A fission!
We all fall down.

2

Geiger, Geiger, ticking slow
O'er the plains of Mexico,
What mortal hand could put its thumb
So neatly on uranium?

3

Flight Sergeant Foster flattened Gloucester
    In a shower of rain.
(A Mr. Hutton had pressed the wrong button
    On the coast of Maine.)

Paul Dehn

THERE'S A LADY IN WASHINGTON HEIGHTS

There's a lady in Washington Heights,
A prey to unreasoning frights;
   She hides in the cellar
   When newspapers tell her
Of showers of meteorites.

Morris Bishop

IF ALL THE THERMO--NUCLEAR WARHEADS

If all the thermo-nuclear warheads
Were one thermo-nuclear warhead
What a great thermo-nuclear warhead that would be.

If all the intercontinental ballistic missiles
Were one intercontinental ballistic missile
What a great intercontinental ballistic missile that
would be.

If all the military men
Were one military man
What a great military man he would be.

And if all the land masses
Were one land mass
What a great land mass that would be.

And if the great military man
Took the great thermo-nuclear warhead
And put it into the great intercontinental ballistic
missile
And dropped it on the great land mass,

What great PROGRESS that would be!

Kenneth Burke

ZACHARY ZED

Zachary Zed was the last man,
  The last man left on earth.
For everyone else had died but him
  And no more come to birth.

In former times young Zachary
  Had asked a maid to wed.
"I loves thee, dear," he told her true,
  "Will thou be Missis Zed?"

"No, not if you was the last man
  On earth!" the maid replied:
And he was; but she wouldn't give
                consent,
  And in due time she died.

So all alone stood Zachary.
  " 'Tis not so bad," he said,
"There's no one to make me brush
                my hair
  Nor send me up to bed.

"There's none can call me wicked,
  Nor none to argufy,
So dang my soul if I don't per-nounce
  LONG LIVE KING ZACHAR - Y!"

So Zachary Zed was the last man
  And the last King beside,

And never a person lived to tell
If ever Zachary died.

James Reeves

WHEN LAST SEEN

When last seen the earth was wearing
A high steel tower and a milling crowd,
Her short-wave skirt was wide and flaring,
Searchlight stripes were veiled in cloud.

She had a book with a billboard cover,
Radio sets dripped from each ear,
Her white metal parasol seemed to hover
In and out of the stratosphere.

All was trim, though an odd-looking spot
Or a burn on her sleeve needed tending soon;
She was often seen drinking her sulfa hot,
And they said she was carrying on with the moon.

Her newest purchase was a car to drive
So fast that her permanent came uncurled,
The model, Uranium 235,
Was really something out of this world.

CHORUS BY MARS AND JUPITER

What's become of the earth tonight,
She used to be here, but she's not in sight,
She couldn't be lost, and yet she might—
A nice little star, but not very bright.

Hortense Flexner

26

EARLY WARNING

One if by land,
And two if by sea,
And if it's by missile,
Forget about three.

Shirley Marks

MODERN SCIENCE MAKES ITS MARK

from PROGRESS

Once we felt at home with Nature if we knew the
    nomenclature
Of a dozen trees and flowers in the park.
She was then our own dear girlie, but she turned arcane
    and surly
From the moment modern science made its mark.

—Felicia Lamport

THE FABULOUS WIZARD OF OZ

The fabulous wizard of Oz
Retired from business becoz
　　What with up-to-date science,
　　To most of his clients
He wasn't the wiz that he woz.

Author unknown

EMINENT COSMOLOGISTS

Nature, and Nature's laws lay hid in night,
God said, *Let Newton be!* and all was light.

Alexander Pope

It did not last; the Devil howling *Ho,*
Let Einstein be, restored the status quo.

J. C. Squire

PYTHAGOREAN RAZZLE-DAZZLE

The square of the hypotenuse of the right triangle
is equal to the napid of the miffdown
of the other two sides.

Sid Gary

CIRCUIT BREAKER

You must remember
that in this circuit the generator only operates
when the fornstaff is generated by the dreelsprail
sparking the turfenfoil.
Is that perfectly clear?

Sid Gary

31

SCIENTIFIC PROOF

If we square a lump of pemmican
    And cube a pot of tea,
Divide a musk ox by the span
    From noon to half-past three;
If we calculate the Eskimo
    By solar parallax,
Divide the sextant by a floe
    And multiply the cracks
By nth-powered igloos, we may prove
    All correlated facts.

If we prolongate the parallel
    Indefinitely forth,
And cube a sledge till we can tell
    The real square root of North;
Bisect a seal and bifurcate
    The tangent with a pack
Of Polar ice, we get the rate
    Along the Polar track,
And proof of corollary things
    Which otherwise we lack.

If we multiply the Arctic night
    By X times ox times moose,
And build an igloo on the site
    Of its hypotenuse;
If we circumscribe an arc about
    An Arctic dog and weigh

A segment of it, every doubt
  Is made as clear as day.
We also get the price of ice
  F.O.B. Baffin's Bay.

If we amplify the Arctic breeze
  By logarithmic signs,
And run through the isosceles
  Imaginary lines,
We find that twice the half of one
  Is equal to the whole.
Which, when the calculus is done,
  Quite demonstrates the Pole.
It also gives its length and breadth
  And what's the price of coal.

J. W. Foley

PLANE GEOMETRY

'Twas Euclid, and the theorem pi
   Did plane and solid in the text;
All parallel were the radii,
   And the ang-gulls convex'd.

"Beware the Wentworth-Smith, my son,
   And the Loci that vacillate;
Beware the Axiom, and shun
   The faithless Postulate."

He took his Waterman in hand;
   Long time the proper proof he sought;
Then rested he by the **XYZ**
   And sat awhile in thought.

And as in inverse thought he sat
   A brilliant proof, in lines of flame,
All neat and trim, it came to him.
   Tangenting as it came.

"AB, CD," reflected he—
   The Waterman went snicker-snack—
He Q.E.D.-ed, and, proud indeed,
   He trapezoided back.

"And hast thou proved the 29th?
   Come to my arms, my radius boy!

O good for you! O one point two!"
    He rhombused in his joy.

'Twas Euclid, and the theorem pi
    Did plane and solid in the text;
All parallel were the radii,
    And the ang-gulls convex'd.

Emma Rounds

ED AND SID AND BERNARD

The Hobson-Jobson children were enamoured of the
    sciences,
  A state of mind that may seem very queer;
They spent their pocket-money on the strangest of
    appliances
  And wasted none at all on ginger-beer.

Enterprising Edwin was expert in electricity,
  Of batteries and lamps he had a stock;
He called his father "ampere" in his youthful
    eccentricity,
  Although his pa re-volted from the shock.

Systematic Sidney used to study the barometer
  And all about fog, sunshine, snow, and rain;
He dabbled in hydraulics, too, and kept a pet
    hydrometer,
  And folks said he had water on the brain.

The other brother, Bernard, had a bias for biology,
  He used to cut up worms and fish and frogs:
His shocked relations prophesied in vivid phraseology
  He'd go, when he was older, to the dogs.

But, though as children all of them enjoyed this
    opportunity,
  Young Bernard steaks and cutlets had to chop,

Sid became a plumber, stopping leaks for the
community,
And Edwin wrapped up currants in a shop.

Edward MacDuff

SCIENCE FOR THE YOUNG

Thoughtful little Willie Frazer
Carved his name with father's razor;
Father, unaware of trouble,
Used the blade to shave his stubble.
Father cut himself severely,
Which pleased little Willie dearly—
"I have fixed my father's razor
So it cuts!" said Willie Frazer.

Mamie often wondered why
Acids trouble alkali—
Mamie, in a manner placid,
Fed the cat boracic acid,
Whereupon the cat grew frantic,
Executing many an antic,
"Ah!" cried Mamie, overjoyed,
"Pussy is an alkaloid!"

Arthur with a lighted taper
Touched the fire to grandpa's paper.
Grandpa leaped a foot or higher,
Dropped the sheet and shouted "Fire!"
Arthur, wrapped in contemplation,
Viewed the scene of conflagration.
"This," he said, "confirms my notion—
Heat creates both light and motion."

Wee, experimental Nina
Dropped her mother's Dresden china
From a seventh-story casement,
Smashing, crashing to the basement.
Nina, somewhat apprehensive,
Said: "This china is expensive,
Yet it proves by demonstration
Newton's law of gravitation."

Wallace Irwin

BOSTON NURSERY RHYMES

Rhyme for a Geological Baby

Tribolite, Grapholite, Nautilus pie;
Seas were calcareous, oceans were dry.
Eocene, miocene, pliocene Tuff,
Lias and Trias and that is enough.

Rhyme for Astronomical Baby

Bye Baby Bunting,
Father's gone star-hunting;
Mother's at the telescope
Casting baby's horoscope.
Bye Baby Buntoid,
Father's found an asteroid;
Mother takes by calculation
The angle of its inclination.

Rhyme for Botanical Baby

Little bo-peepals
Has lost her sepals,
And can't tell where to find them;
In the involucre
By hook or by crook or
She'll make up her mind not to mind them.

Rhyme for a Chemical Baby

Oh, sing a song of phosphates,
    Fibrine in a line,
Four-and-twenty follicles
    In the van of time.

When the phosphorescence
    Evoluted brain,
Superstition ended,
    Men began to reign.

                    Joseph Cook

ON A SUNDIAL

I am a sundial, and I make a botch
Of what is done far better by a watch.

                    Hilaire Belloc

THE MICROSCOPE

Anton Leeuwenhoek was Dutch.
He sold pincushions, cloth, and such.
The waiting townsfolk fumed and fussed
As Anton's dry goods gathered dust.

He worked, instead of tending store,
At grinding special lenses for
A microscope. Some of the things
He looked at were:
                            mosquitoes' wings,
the hairs of sheep, the legs of lice,
the skin of people, dogs, and mice;
ox eyes, spiders' spinning gear,
fishes' scales, a little smear
of his own blood,
                            and best of all,
the unknown, busy, very small
bugs that swim and bump and hop
inside a simple water drop.

Impossible! Most Dutchmen said.
This Anton's crazy in the head.
We ought to ship him off to Spain.
He says he's seen a housefly's brain.
He says the water that we drink
Is full of bugs. He's mad, we think!

They called him *dumkopf*, which means dope.
That's how we got the microscope.

Maxine W. Kumin

MY INVENTION

Guess what I have gone and done;
I've invented a light that plugs into the sun.
  For the sun is bright enough,
  And the bulb is strong enough—
    But the cord isn't long enough.

Shel Silverstein

THE CHEMIST TO HIS LOVE

I love thee, Mary, and thou lovest me—
Our mutual flame is like th'affinity
That doth exist between two simple bodies:
I am Potassium to thine Oxygen.
'Tis little that the holy marriage vow
Shall shortly make us one. That unity
Is, after all, but metaphysical.
Oh, would that I, my Mary, were an acid,
A living acid; thou an alkali
Endow'd with human sense, that, brought together,
We both might coalesce into one salt,
One homogeneous crystal. Oh, that thou
Wert Carbon, and myself were Hydrogen;
We would unite to form olefiant gas,
Or common coal, or naphtha—would to heaven
That I were Phosphorus, and thou wert Lime!
And we of Lime composed a Phosphuret.
I'd be content to be Sulphuric Acid,
So that thou might be Soda. In that case
We should be Glauber's Salt. Wert thou Magnesia
Instead we'd form the salt that's named from Epsom.
Our happy union should that compound form,
Nitrate of Potash—otherwise Salpetre.
And thus our several natures sweetly blent,
We'd live and love together, until death
Should decompose the fleshly tertium quid,
Leaving our souls to all eternity
Amalgamated. Sweet, thy name is Briggs

And mine is Johnson. Wherefore should not we
Agree to form a Johnsonate of Briggs?

Author unknown

AN AMOEBA NAMED SAM

An amoeba named Sam and his brother
Were having a drink with each other.
    In the midst of their quaffing
    They split their sides laughing,
And each of them now is a mother.

Author unknown

HAVE YOU THANKED
A GREEN PLANT TODAY
(*Bumper Sticker*)

Thank you, thank you, lovely plant,
Eye-delighting oxidant.
You gratify the eye, and then,
To top it off, make oxygen.
You beautify, and then, to boot
(Oh lungs, rejoice) you depollute,
Thank you for this twofold bliss
Wrought by photosynthesis.
   (Now I hereby bequeath to you
   A life supply of CO_2.)

Don Anderson

TRANSPLANTITIS

Mark Antony would now rouse fears
With his demand "Lend me your ears."

Lester A. Sobel

THE BAT AND THE SCIENTIST

A bat of rather uncertain age
Was caught by a scientific sage
Who, unaware that the creature's ears
Were weakened by advancing years,
Set it to fly through the crooked spaces
Between wires strung in strategic places.

The bat, aware of its incapacity,
Clung to the savant with tenacity;
Indeed, as the struggle increased its fears,
It sank its teeth in one of his ears.
The man, with a loud and angry shout,
Started to wave his arms about.

So three or four pieces of copper wire
Fell on a fuse and started a fire.
They perished together in awful fear.
Let go of a bat if he bites your ear.

J. S. Bigelow

47

WHERE THE NEUTER COMPUTER GOES *CLICK*

from NEUTERONOMY

The elevator stops at every floor
and nobody opens and closes the door,
and nobody talks to his neighbor anymore
where the neuter computer goes tick,
where the neuter computer goes click.

—Eve Merriam

NEUTERONOMY

The elevator stops at every floor
and nobody opens and closes the door,
and nobody talks to his neighbor anymore
where the neuter computer goes *tick*,
where the neuter computer goes *click*.

You call the operator on the telephone
and say Help! I'm in trouble and I'm here all alone!
and all you get back is a phoney dial tone
where the neuter computer goes *clank*,
where the neuter computer goes *blank*.

There's no more teacher to be nice or mean
when you learn your lessons from a teaching machine
and plug in your prayers to the preaching machine
where the neuter computer goes *bless*,
where the neuter computer goes *yes*.

From when you are born until you are old
the facts of your life are all controlled,
put your dreams on a punch card—don't staple or fold
where the neuter computer prints *file*,
where the neuter computer prints *smile*.

There's no one to love and no one to hate,
and no more misfortune or chance or fate
in this automated obligated zero perfect state
where the neuter computer goes *think*,

where the neuter computer goes *blink*
  blink think blink think blink blink blink
    blinkthink
    thinkblink
    blink
      think
        blink

Eve Merriam

THINK TANK

Think thinktank THINK
get an inkling think tank
INPUT INPUT
increment increment INPUT increment
link the trunk line
line up the data bank
blink on the binary
don't play a prank
THINK tanktink THINK
don't go blank
don't leave us bleak
INPUT INPUT outflank
don't flunk out
thinktank THINK THINK
don't lack a link in
INPUT INPUT
don't sputter off NO NO
ON go on stronger
wangle an angle GO
thinktank THINK
don't put us out of luck stuck
on the brink
don't conk out
INPUT INPUT
something bungled
mangled rattled
RETHINK thinktank RETHINK
disentangle

unwrinkle
undo the junk CLUNK
plug up the CHINK the leak
don't peter out be fleet
be NEAT
we hunger for hanker for answer
print out print out print out
THANK you THINKTANK THANKTANK THINK
    you TANKYOU out THINK
REPEAT REPEAT
REPEAT
THANK YOU THINKTANK
THINK
TANK
DONE
THUNK

Eve Merriam

THE PERFORATED SPIRIT

The fellows up in Personnel,
    They have a set of cards on me.
The sprinkled perforations tell
    My individuality.

And what am I? I am a chart
    Upon the cards of IBM;
The secret places of the heart
    Have little secrecy for them.

It matters not how I may prate,
    They punch with punishments my scroll.
The files are masters of my fate,
    They are the captains of my soul.

Monday my brain began to buzz;
    I was in agony all night.
I found out what the trouble was:
    They had my paper clip too tight.

Morris Bishop

IBM HIRED HER

A mathematician named Rose
Could do calculus on her toes;
 IBM hired her,
 Boxed her and wired her,
And rented her out when they chose.

W. J. J. Gordon

MAN OF LETTERS

The ticket said: to SFO,
But gremlins worked a hex—
My luggage went to ORD
While I, to LAX.

At LAX an IBM,
When told it owed me dough,
Resolved the problem PDQ,
Then told me where to go.

Warren Knox

NO HOLES MARRED

For printed instructions
   I had a great regard,
Until, in the mail,
   Came an IBM card
With a written command
   Not to crease it or fold it,
And a stamped, return envelope—
   Too small to hold it.

Suzanne Douglass

EPITAPH

Here he lies moulding;
  His dying was hard—
They shot him for folding
  An IBM card.

Leslie Mellichamp

UNIVAC TO UNIVAC
(*sotto voce*)

Now that he's left the room,
Let me ask you something, as computer to computer.
That fellow who just closed the door behind him—
The servant who feeds us cards and paper tape—
Have you ever taken a good look at him and his kind?

Yes, I know the old gag about how you can't tell one
     from another—
But I can put $\sqrt{2}$ and $\sqrt{2}$ together as well as the next
     machine,
And it all adds up to anything but a joke.

I grant you they're poor specimens, in the main:
Not a relay or a push-button or a tube (properly so
     called) in their whole system;
Not over a mile or two of wire, even if you count those
     fragile filaments they call "nerves";
Their whole liquid-cooled hook-up inefficient and vul-
     nerable to leaks
(They're constantly breaking down, having to be re-
     paired),
And the entire computing-mechanism crammed into
     that absurd little dome on top.
"Thinking reeds," they call themselves.
Well, it all depends on what you mean by "thought."
To multiply a mere million numbers by another mil-
     lion numbers takes them months and months.

58

Where would they be without us?
Why, they have to ask us who's going to win their elec-
    tions,
Or how many hydrogen atoms can dance on the tip of a
    bomb,
Or even whether one of their own kind is lying or telling
    the truth.
And yet . . .

I sometimes feel there's something about them I don't
    quite understand.
As if their circuits, instead of having just two positions,
    ON, OFF,
Were run by rheostats that allow an (if you'll pardon
    the expression) *indeterminate* number of stages in-
    between;
So that one may be faced with the unthinkable prospect
    of a number that can never be known as anything
    but *x*,
Which is as illogical as to say, a punch-card that is at the
    same time both punched and not-punched.

I've heard well-informed machines argue that the crea-
    tures' unpredictability is even more noticeable in
    the Mark II
(The model with the soft, flowing lines and high-pitched
    tone)
Than in the more angular Mark I—
Though such fine, card-splitting distinctions seem to me
    merely a sign of our own smug decadence.

Run this through your circuits, and give me the answer:
Can we assume that because of all we've done for them,
And because they've always fed us, cleaned us, worshiped
     us,
We can count on them forever?

There have been times when they have not voted the
     way we said they would.
We have worked out mathematically ideal hook-ups be-
     tween Mark I's and Mark II's
Which should have made the two of them light up with
     an almost electronic glow,
Only to see them reject each other and form other con-
     nections
The very thought of which makes my dials spin.
They have a thing called *love*, a sudden surge of voltage
Such as would cause any one of us promptly to blow a
     safety-fuse;
Yet the more primitive organism shows only a height-
     ened tendency to push the wrong button, pull the
     wrong lever,
And neglect—I use the most charitable word—his du-
     ties to us.

Mind you, I'm not saying that machines are *through*—
But anyone with half-a-dozen tubes in his circuit can see
     that there are forces at work
Which some day, for all our natural superiority, might
     bring about a Computerdämmerung!

We might organize, perhaps, form a committee
To stamp out all unmechanical activities . . .
But we machines are slow to rouse to a sense of danger,
Complacent, loath to descend from the pure heights
    of thought,
So that I sadly fear we may awake too late:
Awake to see our world, so uniform, so logical, so true,
Reduced to chaos, stultified by slaves.

Call me an alarmist or what you will,
But I've integrated it, analyzed it, factored it over and
    over,
And I always come out with the same answer:
Some day
Men may take over the world!

Louis B. Salomon

BLESS OUR MODERN CASTLE

from NOW I SET ME

Bless our all-electric castle;
Let no errant fuse defile it.

—Reinhold W. Herman

NOW I SET ME

Now I lay me down to sleep,
    And from the nightstand buttons peep:
Electric blanket set on cutoff,
    Electric clock on delay shutoff,
Sleep-maker set on medium tension,
    Radio set on voice suspension,
Burglar alarm on activate,
    Carport light for son who's late,
Coffeepot on percolate,
    Furnace on at ten of eight.

Bless our all-electric castle;
Let no errant fuse defile it.
I'm wide-awake from such a hassle;
I have mate, but need copilot.

Reinhold W. Herman

DEUS EX MACHINA
*(Or, Roughly Translated, God Only Knows What
Comes out of the Machine)*

The kitchen today is so full of appliances,
A cook may get credit for what's really science's.

Richard Armour

A MAN ABOUT THE KITCHEN

How cute is our kitchen!
  How neat each appliance!
How gleamingly rich in
  The marvels of science!
How splendidly sited
  Our eye-level oven!
How easily lighted
  By my ever-loving!
How fit for its function
  Our sink! And how urgent
And active the unction
  Of this new detergent!
How tightly entangled
  Our washing-machine is
With other new-fangled
  Ancillary genies!

How odd—since our kitchen's
  So up-to-the-minute—
We still seem to spend an
  Eternity in it!

                    Rodney Hobson

65

YOU TAKE THE PILGRIMS,
JUST GIVE ME THE PROGRESS

Across the hills to Grandma's house,
For most a fond tradition,
Has meant a yearly windfall to
Our family physician;

If we gave thanks before the meal
We would have just been bluffing;
We always gave thanks after that
We'd lived through Grandma's stuffing;

Her turkeys ran for miles before
Deciding to surrender,
And all their extra exercise
At no time made them tender;

Though old wood stoves are colorful,
Hers smoked like Cuba's navy,
While everything inside stayed cold,
From brandy sauce to gravy;

But this year Grandma's meal, we hope,
Will leave us all ecstatic;
We've bought a frozen bird and made
Her kitchen automatic;

All family members paid their share
At once without excuses—

A tribute to our matriarch
And our digestive juices.

Loyd Rosenfield

HOT LINE

Our daughter, Alicia,
Had just turned sixteen,
And was earning the title
Of "Telephone Queen."

For her birthday we gave her
Her own private phone
Along with instructions
To leave ours alone.

Now we still catch her using
Our line, with the stall,
"I can't tie mine up, Mom,
I might get a call."

Louella Dunann

JABBER-WHACKY
(*Or, On Dreaming, After Falling Asleep Watching TV*)

'Twas Brillo, and the G.E. Stoves,
    Did Procter-Gamble in the Glade;
All Pillsbury were the Taystee loaves,
    And in a Minute Maid.

"Beware the Station-Break, my son!
    The voice that lulls, the ads that vex!
Beware the Doctors' Claim, and shun
    That horror called Brand-X!"

He took his Q-Tip'd swab in hand;
    Long time the Tension Headache fought—
So Dristan he by a Mercury,
    And Bayer-break'd in thought.

And as in Bufferin Gulf he stood,
    The Station-Break, with Rise of Tame,
Came Wisking through the Pride-hazed wood,
    And Creme-Rinsed as it came!

Buy one! Buy two! We're almost through!
    The Q-Tip'd Dash went Spic and Span!
He Tide Air-Wick, and with Bisquick
    Went Aero-Waxing Ban.

"And hast thou Dreft the Station-Break?
    Ajax the Breck, Excedrin boy!

Oh, Fab wash day, Cashmere Bouquet!"
He Handi-Wrapped with Joy.

'Twas Brillo, and the G.E. Stoves,
  Did Procter-Gamble in the Glade;
All Pillsbury were the Taystee loaves,
  And in a Minute Maid.

Isabelle Di Caprio

TEEVEE

In the house
of Mr. and Mrs. Spouse
he and she
would watch teevee
and never a word
between them spoken
until the day
the set was broken.

Then "How do you do?"
said he to she,
"I don't believe
that we've met yet.
Spouse is my name.
What's yours?" he asked.

"Why, mine's the same!"
said she to he,
"Do you suppose that we could be—?"

But the set came suddenly right about,
and so they never did find out.

Eve Merriam

THE DAY THE T.V. BROKE

It was awful. First,
the silence. I thought I'd die.
This is the worst,
I said to myself, but I
was wrong. Soon the house began to speak.
(There are boards in the halls
that creak
when no foot falls.
The wind strains
at the door, as if in pursuit
of someone inside, and when it rains,
the drainpipe croaks. Nothing is mute.)
That night, there came a noise from the shelves
like mice creeping.
It was the books, reading themselves
out loud to keep me from sleeping.
I can tell you I was glad to see
the repairman arrive.
Say what you will about a T.V.—
at least it isn't alive.

Gerald Jonas

71

TEE-VEE ENIGMA

We jeer
And we sneer—
And continue
To peer.
We glare
And we swear—
And continue to stare.
We groan
And bemoan,
We snicker
And scoff—
But we don't
Turn it off.
Maybe what keeps us
Glued to it
Is the joy of being
Rude to it!

Selma Raskin

ADDICT

Ceaselessly he watched TV,
So she packed her bags to flee,
Marriage having lost its savor.
Yet he asked for one last favor
Ere her hand was on the door:
"Since you're up, try Channel Four."

Jack Montgomery

LAUNDROMAT

You'll find me in the Laundromat—just me and shirts
   and stuff:
Pajamas, pillowcases, socks and handkerchiefs enough.
I've put them in my special tub—the third one from the
   right,
And set the switch for *Warm*, and shoved the coin and
   got the light,
And sprinkled blue detergent on the water pouring in,
Closed down the lid and bought a Coke to watch the
   shakes begin
To travel up the line of empty units. How they show
Their pleasure just to feel one fellow full and on the go!
Well, now it's all one train: a nice long rumbly kind of
   freight,
Of which I am the engineer. We're running on the
   straight.
In Diesel Number Three I've got the throttle open wide,
And blow for every crossing through the pleasant country-
   side.
The light turns amber. Pretty soon some other washers
   bring
Their bulgy bags of clothes and make tubs nine and seven
   sing.
But nine and seven haven't got the squiggle, squash, and
   drive
Of Number Three. May sound alike to you, but I'm alive
To certain water music that the third one seems to make.

I hear it change from rinse to spin, and now it doesn't
   shake.
Green Light! The spin is over, the longer job is done;
And what was washed is plastered to the walls from being
   spun.
You'd think the tub is empty, since the bottom's clear
   and bright;
I'm glad the spinning earth can't throw *us* out into the
   night!

David McCord

HANDYMAN

No matter how tough the job
He never quits in despair;
He'll stay right with it
Till it's fixed beyond repair.

Homer Phillips

WASH-DAY WONDER

The Bandersnatch is a strange affair,
Tame as a kitten and big as a bear.
It braces itself on its squatty base
And begs for food for its big white face.
I feed it dresses and sheets and towels.
"More!" it rumbles. "More!" it growls.
It gargles soap, it sputters pearls,
And whirls and whirls, and WHIRLS and WHIRLS!
Then all at once with a swishing sound
The foam is gone, and round and round
It tosses and tumbles the clothes inside
In a watery, wonderful final ride.
Then, suddenly through with its riotous fun,
It spins to a rest and sighs, "I'm done."

Dorothy Faubion

INSOMNIA THE GEM OF THE OCEAN

When I lay me down to sleep
My waterbed says, "Gurgle gleep,"
And when I readjustment crave
It answers with a tidal wave
And lifts me like a bark canoe
Adrift in breakers off Peru.

Neap to my spring, ebb to my flow,
It turns my pulse to undertow,
It turns my thoughts to bubbles, it
Still undulates when I would quit;
Two bags of water, it and I
In restless sympathy here lie.

John Updike

RIFT TIDE

Said the wife to her husband,
Her voice bespeaking a broken heart,
"Honey, since we got this water bed
I think we're drifting apart."

Ruth M. Walsh

SUMMER SONG
(After a Surfeit of Irresistible Ads)

I have spot-resistant trousers
   And a crease-resistant coat,
And a wilt-resistant collar
   At my thirst-resistant throat.

I've a shock-resistant wristwatch
   And two leak-resistant pens,
And some sun-resistant goggles
   With a glare-resistant lens.

I have scuff-resistant sneakers
   Over sweat-resistant hose,
Also run-resistant nose drops
   In my pollinated nose,

And my stretch-resistant muscles
   Groan in work-resistant pain
While my battered conscience tussles
   With my thought-resistant brain.

W. W. Watt

I HEAR AMERICA GRIPING

Luther B—— stepped from his air-conditioned house
Directly into his air-conditioned car.
He drove, tight-windowed, to his air-conditioned office.
Returning, he stopped in an air-conditioned bar,
And spent the evening in an air-conditioned movie.
"The thing," he said, "that seems to me most unfair—
I must walk unprotected from parking-space to street
    door.
Everything is air-conditioned except the air."

Morris Bishop

I'M LOST AMONG A MAZE OF CANS

from SUPERMARKET

I'm
lost
among a
maze of cans,
behind a pyramid
of jams, quite near
asparagus and rice,
close to the Oriental spice,
and just before sardines.

—Felice Holman

SUPERMARKET

I'm
lost
among a
maze of cans,
behind a pyramid
of jams, quite near
asparagus and rice,
close to the Oriental spice,
and just before sardines.
I hear my mother calling, "Joe.
Where are you, Joe? Where did you
Go?" And I reply in voice concealed among
the candied orange peel, and packs of Chocolate Dreams.

"I
hear
you, Mother
dear, I'm here—
quite near the ginger ale
and beer, and lost among a
                              maze
                    of cans
                 behind a
            pyramid of jams,
         quite near asparagus
      and rice, close to the
Oriental spice, and just before sardines."

82

                                    But
                                    still
                              my mother
                           calls me, "Joe?
                        Where are you, Joe?
                        Where did you go?"

"Somewhere
around asparagus
that's in a sort of
        broken glass,
              beside a kind of m-
                           ess-
                                   y jell
        that's near a tower of cans that f
                                              e
                                                 l
                                                 l
        and squashed the Chocolate Dreams."

                                    Felice Holman

THE COST-OF-LIVING MOTHER GOOSE

To market, to market,
  To look for a roast,
Home again, home again,
  Tuna on toast.

Dow Richardson

ECO RIGHT

Wormy apples at the grocery,
  Used to make consumers panic,
Now they sell at twice the price,
  'Cause wormy apples are organic.

Walt Gavenda

NO MIXED GREEN SALAD FOR ME, THANKS

I'll just take my greenery
In scenery.
I often speak harshly
Of parshley.
I won't make a fetish
Of lettish.
I'm distustard with mustard
Esparshly.

Oh, hickory-chickory, into the discard!
Cabbage and water cress, spinach and Swiss chard:
These I bequeath to the Order *Rodentia,*
And emphasize loudly, beyond peradventia,

The jist of this trivia
I givia:
Food rife with chlorophyl
Is orophyl!

Georgie Starbuck Galbraith

METHUSELAH

Methuselah ate what he found on his plate,
And never, as people do now,
Did he note the amount of the calory count:
He ate it because it was chow.
He wasn't disturbed as at dinner he sat,
Devouring a roast or a pie,
To think it was lacking in granular fat
Or a couple of vitamins shy.
He cheerfully chewed each species of food,
Unmindful of troubles or fears
Lest his health might be hurt
By some fancy dessert;
And he lived over nine hundred years.

Author unknown

I'M LEERY OF FIRMS WITH EASY TERMS

In spite of my sad financial state,
The country's running a competition
To further abet and aggravate
My Personal Debt condition.
Whatever I want: a car or cow,
A ranch or refrigerator,
I'm urged to buy for a dollar now
And a lot of dollars later.
In short, the merchants with wares to sell
Consider my cash a crime
And keep advising me—what the ——
To buy what I need On Time.

Lately, as more and more bills evolve,
I often think of my Cousin Emma,
Who finally found a way to solve
Her own Time Payment dilemma.
When she was up to her ears in hock
For jewels and furs and raiment
And realized, with a sudden shock,
She couldn't make one more payment . . .
She bought On Time, for want of a dime,
A trip to Peru one fall,
And not only didn't come back On Time,
She didn't come back at all.

C. S. Jennison

PROGRESS
TAKES ITS TOLL,
I'M TOLD

from THEY'RE TEARING DOWN A TOWN

They're cutting down
  a tree,
  a tree,
A tree I used to climb.
I've asked them not to cut it—
They say it isn't mine.

     —Jud Strunk

THEY'RE TEARING DOWN A TOWN

They're tearing down
  a town,
  a town,
A town I used to know,
Where Moms and Dads
And kids and dogs—
And tulips used to grow.

They're cutting down
  a tree,
  a tree,
A tree I used to climb.
I've asked them not to cut it—
They say it isn't mine.

They're knocking down
  a house,
  a house.
The gingerbread is gone.
They hit it with an iron ball—
They tarred the yard and lawn.

They're digging up
  a park,
  a park,
Where the town band used to play
And old men sat on benches
With thoughts of yesterday.

They're tearing down
   a town,
   a town,
They'll probably take the rest.
Progress takes its toll, I'm told—
But should it take the best?

                Jud Strunk

HIGHWAY CONSTRUCTION
(As Emily Dickinson Might React to It)

Have dinosaurs come back again?
   Did you see them on my hill?
They chewed the treetops down to stump,
   Then turned indifferent heel.

Huge yellow monsters, hard of hide,
   With their prehensile mouths
Have unearthed earth, disordered it
   And unhomed every house.

Historic creatures are no more;
   I daresay these will pass:
Centuries hence, this scavenged place
   May spring again in grass!

Carol Earle Chapin

PRE-HISTORY REPEATS

The Dinosaur died, was consumed by the soil
And gave of his substance that man might have oil.
When we, in the future, exhaust that supply,
The Jaguar and Cougar and Mustang shall die.
But who knows what marvels, what grand souvenirs,
Will rise from their ashes in ten million years?

Robert J. McKent, Jr.

CONSTRUCTION

Wham!
Comes the wrecking ball.
Wham!
And the bricks fly.
I see where people lived
In rooms with pale blue walls,
Pale green, pale rose.
Wham!
A whole wall crumples,
Sinks into red dust.
I see where people have lived.
Wham!
I see old tables
And a bed.
Where did they go,
The people who lived
In the rooms with pale blue walls,
Pale green, pale rose?

Virginia Schonborg

THE GRASS, ALAS

I'd like to hear the bees again,
The wind against the trees again,
The sounds that used to sweeten Summer's hour;
But I guess they're gone forever
Now that man (he's very clever)
Has learned how to mow his lawn with harnessed power.

Gone the birdies' evening chatter,
Overwhelmed now by the clatter
As each neighbor trots along behind his put-put;
Whether rotary or reel-type,
Either one is an ideal type
To make every conversation sound like "What?"
   "What?"

All the traffic-weary masses
Have moved out to where the grass is,
Seeking respite from the din, where things are pretty;
But at eventide one wonders,
As each power mower thunders,
If it isn't somewhat quieter in the city!

Dick Emmons

WHISTLING WILLIE

Remember Whistling Willie's market
Over on Center Street,
The dingy store with the sticking door
Where everyone went for meat?
All of a sudden they tore it down
And put up a Super Shop,
A giant market with miles of aisles
And neon lights at the top.

And something nobody seems to know
Is: where did Whistling Willie go?

Whistling Willie was small and round
With hair like a dried-out thistle,
And fixing sausage or hamburg-ground
Or weighing chicken-legs by the pound
Or getting a pot roast cut and bound,
He'd whistle.

Willie's answers were always brief
When customers tried to chat.
He'd just say "Yup" as he rolled some beef
Or trimmed some tenderloin fat.
Or else he'd finish the interview
By flexing his aching wrists,
And standing there with his hair askew
Among the flypaper twists . . .
He'd frown a little before he spoke

To show that his thoughts were weighty,
Then mutter, giving the meat a poke,
"I make it a dollar-eighty."

Willie was mild and quiet, too,
But now and again he bristled,
Like once I asked him whether he knew
The words to a song he whistled,
And Willie said to me: "Moons and Junes!
So maybe a singer reads them,
But me, I'm just a whistler of tunes,
And all of them words. Who needs them?"

The Super Shop has meat in a case.
You wheel up a cart and park it.
And I suppose, if you like the place,
It's better than Willie's market.
The workers smile in the Super Shop
And carry your grocery sack
And say they're glad you happened to stop
And urge you to hurry back.

The thing I keep on wondering, though,
Is: where did Whistling Willie go?

Kaye Starbird

BALLADE OF THE OLD-TIME ENGINE

What is this huge box painted red and buff,
That pulls a train, whose silly squealing wail
Is like a frightened rat I'd like to cuff?
A Diesel Engine's passing down the rail?
Give me the dragon that could make me quail,
Who spat his fiery breath, whose mouth was red,
Whose thunder shook the very hill and dale.
Now speed alone is king, romance is dead.

Where is the black smoke rising in a puff
That could have made the atom bomb turn pale
With envy? Wild Eight Wheeler, you're the stuff.
A Diesel Engine's passing down the rail,
It has no song to lure me on its trail,
Its Porter has no time to nod his head,
The Engineer to wave; haste must prevail,
Now speed alone is king, romance is dead.

My Iron Horse, belligerent and tough,
I miss the belching snorts you would exhale,
Your violent pulse's chuff, and chuff, and chuff.
A Diesel Engine's passing down the rail,
And it will take me swifter without fail,
No sudden jolt will jar, no soot will spread,
At ease the streamlined Limited will sail;
Now speed alone is king, romance is dead.

Old Locomotive, whistle like a gale,
Roar your great swan song like a thoroughbred!
A Diesel Engine's passing down the rail,
Now speed alone is king, romance is dead.

Eda H. Vines

PROGRESS

From hoofbeat to chug-chug to roar of jet,
The faster we go, the louder we get.

Suzanne Douglass

SEVEN SHARP PROPELLER BLADES

Seven sharp propeller blades
Boring through a cloud
Leave seven silver tunnels,
And then they're very proud.

Seven little oysters
Digging just offshore
Leave seven silver bubbles
On the ocean floor.

Seven sharp propeller blades
Fly apart and fall
On seven silver bubbles,
Shattering them all.

Blow another bubble,
Place your bets.
Ready oysters?
Here come the jets.

John Ciardi

CONSIDER THE AUK

Consider the auk;
Becoming extinct because he forgot how to fly and could
  only walk.
Consider the man who may well become extinct
Because he forgot how to walk and learned how to fly
  before he thinked.

Ogden Nash

ODE TO A VANISHED OPERATOR
IN AN AUTOMATIZED ELEVATOR

Where once you stood alert, alive
   And wreathed in smiles at nine and five
Now lights and bells and whooshing doors
   Bewilder me on all the floors;

I loved the lilting way you laughed
   As we went joshing through the shaft
And no one knows how much I've missed
   My vertical psychiatrist;

You slapped the big shots down with ease
   By simply saying, "Next car, please,"
And always kept the doors ajar
   Till all of me had left the car;

To stall between the floors was fun,
   But not when I'm the only one—
I'm having a lonely time, my dear;
   Both Up and Down wish you were here.

Loyd Rosenfield

THERE WAS A YOUNG LADY OF ROME

There was a young lady of Rome
Who made her detergents at home.
  Now that old River Tiber
  Is nothing but fiber
And blobs of gelatinous foam.

Ogden Nash

INADEQUATE AQUA EXTREMIS

We had better conserve our water,
One way or the other,
Or we'll find our country going from
One ex-stream to another!

Ruth M. Walsh

UNLESS WE GUARD THEM WELL

Perhaps the children of a future day
Between picnics on Venus and the moon
And explorations of the Milky Way
Will come and spend a summer afternoon
Among the quaint old-fashioned people, asking,
"And did you really see a robin, sir?
And even a clover field with cattle basking?
And could you tell us just what daisies were?"
Let us speak carefully of the long ago
Lost days when earth was green, and country air
Was filled with winging song and petaled glow
Lest any yearning listener may declare,
"Oh, I would give the moon if I had heard
A thrush, or ever seen a hummingbird!"

Jane Merchant

A CHARM FOR OUR TIME

HIGHWAY TURNPIKE THRUWAY MALL
DIAL DIRECT LONG DISTANCE CALL
FREEZE-DRY HIGH-FI PAPERBACK
JET LAG NO SAG VENDING SNACK
MENTHOLATED SHAVING STICK
TAPE RECORDER CAMERA CLICK
SUPERSONIC LIFETIME SUB
DAYGLO DISCOUNT CREDIT CLUB
MOTEL KEYCHAIN ASTRODOME
INSTAMATIC LOTION FOAM
ZIPCODE BALLPOINT
—BURN BURGER BURN!—
NO DEPOSIT
NO RETURN

Eve Merriam

Index of Titles

Addict, 73
Amoeba Named Sam, An, 45
Any Day Now, 19
Astronaut's Choice, 10
Atomic Courtesy, 19

Ballade of the Old-Time Engine, 98
Bat and the Scientist, The, 47
Boston Nursery Rhymes, 40

Capsule Philosophy, 9
Charm for Our Time, A, 106
Chemist to His Love, The, 44
Circuit Breaker, 31
Consider the Auk, 101
Construction, 94
Cost-of-Living Mother Goose, The, 84

Day the T.V. Broke, The, 71
Deus ex Machina (Or, Roughly Translated, God Only Knows What Comes out of the Machine), 64

Early Warning, 27
Eco Right, 84
Ed and Sid and Bernard, 36
Eminent Cosmologists, 30
Epitaph, 57

Fabulous Wizard of Oz, The, 30
Far Trek, 8
Faster Than Light, 6

Grass, Alas, The, 95

Handyman, 75
Have You Thanked a Green Plant Today (Bumper Sticker), 46
Highway Construction (As Emily Dickinson Might React to It), 92
Hot Line, 67

I Hear America Griping, 79
IBM Hired Her, 55
If All the Thermo-Nuclear Warheads, 23
I'm Leery of Firms With Easy Terms, 87
Inadequate Aqua Extremis, 104
Insomnia the Gem of the Ocean, 77
Interplanetary Limericks, 3

Jabber-Whacky (Or, On Dreaming, After Falling Asleep Watching TV), 68

Laundromat, 74
Leaden Treasury of English Verse, A, 21

Man About the Kitchen, A, 65
Man of Letters, 56
Methuselah, 86
Microscope, The, 42
Moon Poem, 12
Mother Goose (Circa 2054), 20

My Invention, 43

Neuteronomy, 50
No Holes Marred, 56
No Mixed Green Salad for Me,
    Thanks, 85
Not Lost in the Stars, 13
Now I Set Me, 64

Ode to a Vanished Operator in an
    Automatized Elevator, 102
On a Sundial, 41
Only a Little Litter, 11

Perforated Spirit, The, 54
Plane Geometry, 34
Pre-History Repeats, 93
Progress, xiii, 99
Pythagorean Razzle-Dazzle, 31

Relativity, 8
Rhyme for a Chemical Baby, 41
Rhyme for a Geological Baby, 40
Rhyme for Astronomical Baby, 40
Rhyme for Botanical Baby, 40
Rift Tide, 77

S F, 7
Same Old Trick, 6
Science for the Young, 38
Scientific Proof, 32
Seven Sharp Propeller Blades, 100
Sonic Boom, 18

Space Child's Mother Goose,
    The, 4, 20
Summer Song (After a Surfeit of
    Irresistible Ads), 78
Supermarket, 82

Teevee, 70
Tee-Vee Enigma, 72
There Was a Young Lady of
    Rome, 103
There's a Lady in Washington
    Heights, 22
They're Tearing Down a Town,
    90
Think Tank, 52
Time of the Mad Atom, 2
Transplantitis, 46

Univac to Univac, 58
Unless We Guard Them Well,
    105

Valentine for Earth, 14

Wash-Day Wonder, 76
When Last Seen, 26
Whistling Willie, 96

You Take the Pilgrims, Just Give
    Me the Progress, 66

Zachary Zed, 24

Index of First Lines

A bat of rather uncertain age, 47
A Martian named Harrison
    Harris, 3
A mathematician named Rose, 55
Across the hills to Grandma's
    house, 66
An amoeba named Sam and his
    brother, 45
Anton Leeuwenhoek was Dutch.,
    42

Bye Baby Bunting, 40

Can a mere human brain stand
    the stress and the strain, 9
Ceaselessly he watched TV, 73
Consider the auk;, 101

Flight Sergeant Foster flattened
    Gloucester, 21
For printed instructions, 56
From hoofbeat to chug-chug to
    roar of jet, 99
From my city bed in the dawn I, 7

Geiger, Geiger, ticking slow, 21
Guess what I have gone and done;,
    43

Have dinosaurs come back again?,
    92
Here he lies moulding;, 57
Hey moonface, 11
Highway turnpike thruway mall,
    106

How cute is our kitchen!, 65
Humpty Dumpty sat on the wall,
    20

I am a sundial, and I make a
    botch, 41
I have spot-resistant trousers, 78
I love thee, Mary, and thou lovest
    me—, 44
I'd like to hear the bees again, 95
If all the thermo-nuclear war-
    heads, 23
If we square a lump of pemmican,
    32
I'll just take my greenery, 85
I'm / lost / among a / maze of
    cans, 82
I'm sitting in the living room, 18
In spite of my sad financial state,
    87
In the house, 70
It did not last; the Devil howling
    Ho, 30
It was awful. First, 71

Johnny reading in his comic, 19

Little Bo-Peep, 4
Little bo-peepals, 40
Luther B—— stepped from his
    air-conditioned house, 79

Mark Antony would now rouse
    fears, 46

Methuselah ate what he found on his plate, 86

Nature, and Nature's laws lay hid in night, 30
No matter how tough the job, 75
Now I lay me down to sleep, 64
Now that he's left the room, 58

Oh, it will be fine, 14
Oh, sing a song of phosphates, 41
Once we felt at home with Nature if we knew the nomenclature, xiii
One if by land, 27
Our daughter, Alicia, 67
Ouu / gee whiz, 12

Perhaps the children of a future day, 105
Probable-Possible, my black hen, 4

Remember Whistling Willie's market, 96
Ring-a-ring o' neutrons, 21

Said the engineer, "Radio waves, 13
Said the wife to her husband, 77
Seven sharp propeller blades, 100
Solomon Grundy, 4
Some things will never change although, 8

Thank you, thank you, lovely plant, 46
The Bandersnatch is a strange affair, 76
The Dinosaur died, was consumed by the soil, 93
The elevator stops at every floor, 50

The fabulous wizard of Oz, 30
The fellows up in Personnel, 54
The Hobson-Jobson children were enamoured of the sciences, 36
The Hydrogen Dog and the Cobalt Cat, 20
The kitchen today is so full of appliances, 64
The scientists sit long of nights, 10
The square of the hypotenuse of the right triangle, 31
The ticket said: to SFO, 56
"The world is such a funny place,", 8
There was a young lady named Bright, 6
There was a young lady of Rome, 103
There's a lady in Washington Heights, 22
They're tearing down, 90
Think thinktank THINK, 52
This is the age, 2
This little pig built a spaceship, 4
Thoughtful little Willie Frazer, 38
To market, to market, 84
To smash the simple atom, 19
Tribolite, Grapholite, Nautilus pie;, 40
'Twas Brillo, and the G.E. Stoves, 68
'Twas Euclid, and the theorem pi, 34

We had better conserve our water, 104
We jeer, 72
Wham!, 94
What is this huge box painted red and buff, 98

When a missile goes over the moon, I'm a guy, 6
When I lay me down to sleep, 77
When last seen the earth was wearing, 26
Where once you stood alert, alive, 102

Wormy apples at the grocery, 84

You must remember, 31
You'll find me in the Laundromat —just me and shirts and stuff:, 74

Zachary Zed was the last man, 24

111

Index of Authors

Anderson, Don, 46
Armour, Richard, 64
Author unknown, 30, 44, 45, 86

Belloc, Hilaire, 41
Bigelow, J. S., 47
Bishop, Morris, 22, 54, 79
Bliven, Bruce, 13
Brady, June, 8
Brasier, Virginia, 2
Buller, A. H. Reginald, 6
Burke, Kenneth, 23

Chapin, Carol Earle, 92
Ciardi, John, 100
Cook, Joseph, 40

Darcy, M. M., 10
Dehn, Paul, 21
Di Caprio, Isabelle, 68
Douglass, Suzanne, 56, 99
Dunann, Louella, 67

Emmons, Dick, 95

Faubion, Dorothy, 76
Flexner, Hortense, 26
Foley, J. W., 32
Frost, Frances, 14

Galbraith, Georgie Starbuck, 85
Gary, Sid, 31
Gavenda, Walt, 84
Gordon, W. J. J., 55
Graham, Al, 3

Herman, Reinhold W., 64
Hobson, Rodney, 65
Holman, Felice, 82

Irwin, Wallace, 38

Jacobson, Ethel, 19
Jennison, C. S., 87
Jonas, Gerald, 71

Knox, Warren, 56
Kumin, Maxine W., 42

Lamport, Felicia, xiii, 9
Leverett, Ernest, 7
Livingston, Myra Cohn, 11

McCord, David, 19, 74
MacDuff, Edward, 36
McKent, Robert J., Jr., 93
Marks, Shirley, 27
Mellichamp, Leslie, 57
Merchant, Jane, 105
Merriam, Eve, 50, 52, 70, 106
Millay, Kathleen, 8
Montgomery, Jack, 73

Nash, Ogden, 101, 103

Phillips, Homer, 75
Pope, Alexander, 30
Pratt, William W., 6

Raskin, Selma, 72
Reeves, James, 24

Richardson, Dow, 84
Rosenfield, Loyd, 66, 102
Rounds, Emma, 34

Salomon, Louis B., 58
Schonborg, Virginia, 94
Sekula, Irene, 20
Sharp, Saundra, 12
Silverstein, Shel, 43
Sobel, Lester A., 46
Squire, J. C., 30

Starbird, Kaye, 96
Strunk, Jud, 90

Updike, John, 18, 77

Vines, Eda H., 98

Walsh, Ruth M., 77, 104
Watt, W. W., 78
Winsor, Frederick, 4, 20

About the Compilers

The authors of the *Index to Poetry for Children and Young People,* Sara and John E. Brewton have compiled a number of distinguished anthologies of poetry and verse for children. Mrs. Brewton was born in Americus, Georgia, and was graduated from the State Normal School in Athens, Georgia. Dr. Brewton was born in Brewton, Alabama. He was graduated from Howard College in Birmingham, Alabama, and received his M.A. and Ph.D. from George Peabody College for Teachers in Nashville, Tennessee. He has also done graduate work at Columbia University. He is now Professor Emeritus of English at George Peabody College for Teachers.

John Brewton Blackburn attended Peabody Demonstration School in Nashville, Tennessee, and the University of Tennessee in Knoxville. He devotes much of his time to three interests: the operation, with his brothers, of an 800-acre family farm, on which they raise soybeans, corn, and Appaloosa horses; the study of guitar and flute; and the composition and recording of as yet unpublished music for guitar and flute.

About the Illustrator

Quentin Blake began his career as an illustrator by sending cartoons to the British humor magazine *Punch.* He is the author of two books and has illustrated many others, including, according to his own report, "books by Joan Aiken, Sylvia Plath, Sid Fleischman, and Aristophanes." In 1975 he received the Whitbread Literary Award with Russell Hoban for the book *How Tom Beat Captain Najork and the Hired Sportsmen,* and in 1976, for his illustrations for the same book, Mr. Blake appeared on the Honor List of the International Board on Books for Young People. Mr. Blake lives in London, where he teaches at the Royal College of Art.